NINJA
DEATH
TOUCH

Ninja Death Touch
Copyright 1983 by Ashida Kim

Published by Paladin Press, a division of
Paladin Enterprises, Inc., P.O. Box 1307
Boulder, Colorado 80306

ISBN 0-87364-257-0
Printed in the United States of America

NINJA DEATH TOUCH

ASHIDA KIM

PALADIN PRESS
BOULDER, COLORADO

Also by Ashida Kim:
Secrets of the Ninja

CONTENTS

1. ORIGIN AND BACKGROUND

Nien Jih Ssu Ch'u Chueh is the highly specialized Chinese art of killing without leaving a trace. Literally translated, this means "Ninja Death Touch." To commit such an act, five qualities are required: the will, the strength, the knowledge, the daring, and the silence.

The Death Touch of the Ninja encompasses three major categories: *Dim Ching,* the method of attacking the nerves and nerve plexes of the body; *Dim Hsueh,* the technique of striking the blood vessels and causing blood clots; and *Dim Mak,* the art of manipulating the Chi of the body by hitting the Points of Alarm of the acupuncture system.

To properly strike the vital and fatal points of the body, the student must learn to form his hand into the correct weapon. Some blows require the fist, some the edge of the hand, and others the fingers. All will be explained, and a method of training for each will be given so that the student may experiment with the various methods.

Above all, the Ssu Ch'u Chueh is a way of knowledge. The charts and tables provided are the most complete and pertinent available to Western students. They should be committed to memory. But since the Death Touch implies a certain amount of premeditation, they may be used for reference if that is preferred.

Since the key to these techniques is the accurate delivery of the proper hand weapon to a precise anatomical target at the appropriate time, certain tactical methods from the *Kumi-Uchi* (Ninja Combat System) will be discussed in the final portion of this work.

Not only are these techniques among the most deadly in the entire spectrum of the martial arts, they may be considered medicinal in nature. The art itself was developed as an adjunct to Chinese boxing. In such sports, injuries often result, especially among the unskilled. By knowing which vital points to avoid, injuries could be minimized, learned the Chinese Master boxers. Much as the constant pummeling of the professional boxer can cause those who lead with their chin to become "punch-drunk," or the continued impact of body slams results in kidney problems for the wrestler, so the goal of the Death Touch is the destruction of a specific organ by striking a specific target. When certain cosmological and physiological knowledge is properly integrated with Death Touch technique, the desired effect may occur immediately or with a time delay.

As alluded to above, the classification of the vital and fatal points of the body developed so they could be avoided in friendly competition; and the study of the system was congruent to the development of acupuncture. Inevitably, however, the unscrupulous learned of the implications of such a system and used it for their own immoral purposes. Hence the sordid reputation of the Death Touch.

It should also be mentioned that the need for secrecy among not only those who developed the system, but also those who rose to prominence as assassins, has prompted many misconceptions about the art. Foremost among these is the idea that Dim Mak is the only such system, and that it encompasses *all* of the vital and fatal points. This is far from true. Dim Mak is the most difficult to learn, to be sure, but it is not the only means by which the enemy may be dispatched instantly or at your leisure. Also, certain *ryu,* or schools, specialize in only one or two of these techniques, as sort of a "trademark." The methods given here are those taught to the *chunin,* or middle-level agents, of the *Hai Lung T'ung Pao Ying,* or the Black Dragon Tong of Retribution, the deadliest assassins of the Orient.

We have no fear that the information revealed here for the first time will be misused, since the perfection of a single technique may require a lifetime.

HISTORY OF THE NINJA DEATH TOUCH

It has long been held in the study of Ninjitsu that the Death Touch originated in Tibet. This is consistent with other theories concerning various martial arts. Somewhere in the lost and desolate regions where lie the Himalayas, many mystic and arcane arts were born. The science of the Death Touch was considered ancient even before it began to spread across China and India.

From the beginning, there were three master points which could heal or kill with virtually no pressure or contact at the will of the practitioner. This is the basis for the legends of masters who could kill with no physical contact. Men who learned this skill could "strike a man dead with a glance," or "shoot daggers with their eyes." The three master points—positive, negative, and neutral—were each broken down into three more components for a total of nine lesser points. These require some contact to effect a result and can cure or injure as well as kill. These points are utilized by evangelists who can "heal by the laying on of hands," and were also the basis for Anton Mesmer's magnetic experiments.

By the time the system reached China, it had been further subdivided into eighty-one points, the mechanism for each being based on one of the Five Elements.

Astrological and cosmological considerations were added at this time. This brought the number of vital and fatal points to 108, further lending an air of mysticism to the system.

At various times during the evolution of Japanese and Chinese culture, contact and exchanges have been made by not only the physicians and scholars of both kingdoms, but also the warriors. During the time of the Chinese Triad Societies and the development of the Tong Clans, the criminal elements and espionage networks of the two nations also interacted. By these means the knowledge of the Death Touch came to the Koga clans of Honshu, the large island of the Japanese chain. This area was ruled by no less than fifty clans of Ninja-ryu, some of which consisted of as few as three members (a father and his two sons). Most ryu had thirty or more genin, and five such clans numbered over one hundred strong.

In the fashion of the Triad Society, three jonin ruled each ryu. These jonin could be replaced or ousted, depending on the changing politics of the day. During the numerous "sword hunts" which were meant to stamp out Ninjitsu, the clans were separated, the families exterminated, and many ryu thus expired. Some have allied themselves with other, stronger groups. Some remaining Ninja are *ronin*, who pass on the secrets of their art only to blood relations.

"THE UNWILLING AGENT"

Following is a standard parable taught to each member of the Hai Lung T'ung Pao Ying. It illustrates an actual and successful application of the Ninja Death Touch system as presented in this work. The value of the following tale should be immediately apparent to the reader upon its completion.

During the last half of the sixteenth century in feudal Japan, a time of unrest and conflict between the rival warlords of the era, a certain chunin of the Black Dragon Tong, known as Takashi, was commissioned to assassinate a *daimyo* (nobleman) in a small prefecture slightly to the north of *Edo* (Tokyo).

The agent made his way to the home village of this official and evaluated the situation. This noble of lesser rank was not only impressed enough by his own importance that he affected many trappings of rank, but also surrounded himself with samurai bodyguards twenty-four hours a day. The room in which he slept was the uppermost in a two-story structure, in the front, clearly visible from the numerous sentry posts. No chance existed of poisoning the ruler's food, since security around the kitchen was as strict as that on the upper floor.

The daimyo further seemed to have no pattern to his activities. He never appeared in the same place, and there was no place he went more than once a day at the same time. His schedule was erratic, and his movements were obscured by the craft of his bodyguards.

Takashi's mission required that the lord be killed within one week. He therefore had no time for long reconnaissances. After three days he hit upon a plan. The ninja disguised himself as a ronin and waited for the changing of the guard at a local sake house.

Soldiers—even samurai—being what they are, it was not long before one of the local bodyguards appeared in the neighborhood sake house. From his observations, Takashi recognized the sentry as one who was often boisterous and fond of demonstrating his prowess. Within short order the ninja had engaged him in conversation and drink, until at last the guard was sufficiently agitated and intoxicated to be goaded into a fight.

Since this was a friendly contest, the two grappled about the inn, a place having been cleared in the center of the largest room. The combat was singularly uninteresting, with the guard, Hideo, winning easily.

Takashi congratulated his new comrade-in-arms and bought him yet another flask of sake in celebration. Late in the evening, the pair staggered arm in arm to the street and off into the darkness. Hideo began to complain of a strange pain in his forehead as they lurched along; Takashi merely quickened their pace into the gloom. Notably, his gait and posture were no longer those of a drunken ronin.

At length, they drew near the compound of the daimyo. Hideo succumbed to the influence of the rice wine and became unconscious. Takashi slipped him into a convenient alley, which he had previously prepared as an observation post. He quickly stripped the sentry of his kimono, weapons, and purse. Setting these aside, he knelt over the form of Hideo and pressed the *Nin Chu Tsubo,* a fatal point located one-third of the way down the philtrum, from the base of the nose to the edge of the upper lip. He held the tip of his index finger against this point with a firm, direct pressure for ten seconds, then gradually released, then repeated three times (this point is well known in acupuncture for the treatment of epilepsy). He rubbed the wrists and neck of the unconscious bodyguard and stirred him awake.

When he was sure Hideo was lucid enough to comprehend his actions, Takashi slapped him across the face and laughed loudly. Rising and turning his back on the guard, he began gathering up his possessions as if to leave.

Though Hideo was groggy, he grew dimly aware that he was being robbed. He would spring up and kill this upstart who dared to steal from the daimyo's bodyguard! But his arms and legs were leaden. In fact, the more he attempted to move, the less chance there seemed of his doing so. A clammy sweat appeared on the brow of Hideo, who had always been so proud of his physical power. He could not move so much as a finger!

His eyes alone he could use, and with them he saw the ronin stealing Hideo's two swords, as well as his kimono. The fact that he was naked only intensified his sense of vulnerability. But that warrior spirit, which drove the samurai to many amazing deeds, felt only anger, hatred at being duped. Hideo's mind roared with rage, but his voice was only a whisper. Again he screamed, and once more only a shadow of his voice crept out.

Takashi turned, still laughing softly, and looked into the eyes of Hideo. He read the anger and frustration, as well as the hopelessness.

"So, Master Bodyguard, you are awake! Good! Your purse is light, my friend. No matter, it will do well enough for Takashi the Thief." He laughed again.

"I see that you are wondering why you cannot move, my friend. It is a trick I learned from a ninja. While we wrestled I merely pressed a spot on the back of your neck. After a time, this attack causes the victim to become paralyzed. At first it is only the muscles which cannot be used, but in three days, the heart will cease its beating and you will die. Of course, you will go mad long before then . . . ." The ninja smiled at the paralyzed sentry and rose as if to leave.

"No . . . ," whimpered the once mighty Hideo.

"No you say?" replied Takashi, kneeling once more over his victim. "No? And why not? What have you, Master Bodyguard, that will make your life worth more to me than your scanty purse?"

There was no reply.

"Come now, if you have no treasures of your own, perhaps your master? Surely he would not miss a few trinkets in exchange for the life of his personal guard?"

Hideo considered this for a moment. His eyes darted back and forth, he licked his lips. They were dry in spite of the perspiration on his face, which lent a chilling effect to the scene as it evaporated in the cool night air. To be left here naked, thought Hideo, paralyzed to die in three days, the victim of a simple thief! The shame of it!

Takashi muttered and stood over Hideo, "I thought not." The ninja turned to leave.

"Wait," whispered the sentry.

The ninja made him call twice more before he returned. Each time the voice of Hideo became more plaintive and compliant.

"You have the cure?" asked Hideo.

"I can reverse the effects if I choose," replied Takashi. "What do you offer?"

"In my master's chamber . . . a small jewel chest . . . it is just inside the shoji to his room . . . on the right side."

"Ha! Do you take me for a fool? The house is crawling with guards. Your master is never alone. How could one enter his bed chamber?"

"Only at the time," gasped Hideo," when my master is with his mistress—a girl from the village. She is brought to him every night . . . at the Hour of the Dog (11 P.M.–1 A.M.) . . . ."

"How?"

"She is escorted by the sentry at the main gate. When the daimyo takes her to his private chamber, you would be alone with the jewel chest . . . until she has to be taken away."

Takashi had seen the girl approach the gate on previous evenings. She gave all appearances of a kitchen worker, although he had noted that she was not unattractive. He had also seen that the main gate guard was always replaced shortly after he went inside. He decided to try a desperate plan.

"You have done well, Master Bodyguard. All had best be as you have described, for your very life depends on my safe return." He shed his clothes and accoutrements and quickly dressed in his ninja garb. Over this he wore Hideo's kimono. Throwing one more smile in the direction of the helpless samurai, Takashi made for the gate.

Takashi carried the two swords of Hideo as he approached the gate sentry. He staggered and lurched, reeling drunkenly along the path. All the while his sharp eyes noted the passing of each sentry on duty, as well as the locations of all the posted guards. He fell flat on his face in front of the gate sentry, who naturally bent over what he mistakenly recognized as one of his off-duty brothers who had imbibed a bit too much.

The sentry died silently as Takashi applied the fingers of his right hand to a certain point on the sentry's throat, and it was no small feat to carry the body to the house while making it appear that the sentry was aiding his drunken companion. Once inside, Takashi discarded the kimono of Hideo and donned the sentry's uniform over his "suit of darkness." Concealing the body, Takashi returned to the gate and took up the sentry's position.

He knew from previous evenings that the guards were not due to change shifts during the appointed hour, so he merely waited until the girl presented herself for admission and led her inside. Takashi was a skillful ninja, he carefully walked beside the girl, following her as she made her familiar journey upstairs. He waited patiently as she prepared herself by bathing and donning her make-up. At last she was ready.

Takashi followed her to the master's chamber. The guard at the door recognized the mistress and drew the shoji aside as she passed. The daimyo was a fat man, given to excess in every way. He smiled pleasantly as the girl approached him. They walked into the next room, closed the door, and all was silent.

Takashi spent a few minutes exploring the room quietly. He tucked the jewel chest inside the uniform he had worn into the inner sanctum as he removed it. Next he stripped off his night suit and lay it to one side. Once again dressing in the uniform, he slid the door to the hallway open a few inches and signaled the sentry to come in quietly.

Unaccustomed to this turn of events, the guard entered and was immediately and silently killed. Takashi dressed this guard in his night suit and placed his body near the forward window of the room.

By this time, the daimyo and his mistress were deep in the throes of passion. Takashi entered quickly and killed the official with a single blow of the long sword of Hideo. The mistress screamed before the sword arced again through the night air and silenced her forever.

"Murder!" yelled Takashi at the top of his lungs. "The Master has been slain! Sound the alarm! Murder!"

The house was immediately roused as other guards took up the call. Footsteps pounded through the halls and rooms as samurai seized their weapons and ran to their battle stations.

"Assassins!" screamed Takashi, "This way! Ninja! Ninja in the Master's room!" When he heard the other members of the guard nearing, Takashi cried out once more, "Stop! He's going for the window!" With that, he hurled the dead sentry, dressed in his nightsuit, out the window of the chamber. When the other guards entered he was screaming down at the broken form below the window. The other members of the bodyguard detail dashed to look out of the window, while still others surrounded the figure.

"Watch him! It's a trap!" shouted Takashi as he slipped away from the throng and made his way out of the courtyard.

Shortly, he found himself back in the alley with the drunken Hideo.

"Well, my friend, it was as you said. I have the gems. Indeed, your life was worth more than your purse." He knelt beside the paralyzed sentry, lifted him, wrapped his arms around the neck of his unwilling ally, and manipulated the vertebrae to relieve the pressure he had previously induced. Immediately Hideo could feel the life returning to his limbs. He still could not move, but now he felt as if he would soon be able to do so.

"The numbness will be gone in a short time. You will forgive me if I do not remain until you regain your strength. I shall leave your garments and weapons here, as well as this armor which I found it necessary to borrow. Naturally I shall keep your purse." He smiled broadly at the struggling samurai.

"Farewell, Master Bodyguard," said Takashi as he melted into the night.

Hideo gradually regained the use of his limbs and in about an hour returned to the compound. By this time, the ruse had been discovered. Hideo was found in possession of the gate sentry's armor, with the blood of the master on his sword. He was summarily executed.

Takashi collected his fee and returned to the serenity of his home in the Koga province.

2. THE THREE WAYS

The art of the Ninja Death Touch is essentially divided into the Three Ways, any and all of which are capable of inducing death without leaving a trace.

Firstly, the nerves and nerve plexes of the body may be attacked with devastating results. This is known as *Dim Ching.* The blood vessels and blood gates may be attacked, causing severe damage not only at the site of injury, but also to all areas distal to that point. This is called *Dim Hsueh.* Or, the Chi, the vital energy of life, the prana of the Yogis, may be diverted from its orderly flow within the body to hypertonify or sedate a given organ to cause death. This is the legendary *Dim Mak.*

In many cases these points coincide (see Chart A). Such targets are known as "fatal points," since the likelihood that death will ensue is great if these are manipulated appropriately. Each method has its specific uses and applications, these being largely dependent on the wishes and skill of the practitioner. Death may be delayed with any of the techniques given here by varying the power of the strike, and the time at which it is applied.

The purpose of this section is to illustrate how a small amount of force may be properly applied to achieve the maximum effect, and the physiology by which this is accomplished.

A thorough knowledge of human anatomy and physiology is central to the study of the Ninja Death Touch. Pressure points, nerve centers, major blood vessels, and organs are all vulnerable to attack.

The facing Chart A illustrates the location of the major vital areas of the body which are considered primary targets. These points are especially vulnerable to attack by various Death Touch methods.

The abdomen, on which lie many of the vital and fatal points, is divided into two large cavities. The upper cavity, above the diaphragm, contains the lungs and heart. The lower cavity contains the remaining organs. Kidneys are exposed on the dorsal surface. The upper section is known as the pleural cavity, the lower as the thoracic cavity.

1.	Trachea	7.	Upper Liver
2.	Lungs	8.	Lower Liver
3.	Blood Vessel	9.	Large Intestine
4.	Heart	10.	Small Intestine
5.	Diaphragm	11.	Bladder
6.	Stomach	12.	Testicles

⊖ Trachea; esophagus; carotid sheath.

⊜ Branchial artery; (supplies blood to the arm).

⊜ Solar plexus; (at the tip of the xyphoid process).

㊃ Blood vessel supplying the heart.

㊄ Heart; (above the solar plexus).

㊅ Upper lobes of the liver; on the right, the spleen.

㊆ Lower lobes of the liver; on the right, the kidney.

㊇ "Pit" of the stomach; (striking upward).

㊉ Hara; (two inches below the navel).

㊌ Urinary bladder; testicles.

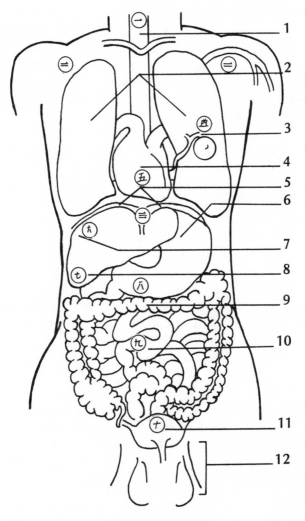

CHART A
Vital and fatal points of the body.

_...ING

Nerve Point Method

The nervous system of the body may be divided into three parts: the autonomic, which controls body functions not under conscious control (i.e., respiration, digestion); the sympathetic, which controls voluntary muscle action; and the parasympathetic, which relays information from the senses to the brain.

Nerves are complex fibers which transmit electro-chemical impulses back and forth from the brain to the body. Nerves to and from all parts of the body are grouped together within the spinal cord. Each area of the brain is concerned with a particular function of the body. Impulses traveling from the cortex pass into the spinal cord and are transmitted to the appropriate peripheral nerve. The electrical impulse is conducted along the axon, an extension of the nerve cell itself. The cell bodies are found in an enlarged cluster known as a ganglion, and are enclosed in a fatty myelin sheath. The function of this covering is to insulate the nerve and accelerate the conduction of nervous signals. This is accomplished by the secretion of a chemical known as acetylcholine.

When the brain signals, the impulse travels to the spinal cord axon. Between this fibrous bundle and the peripheral nerve which will receive the impulse, there is an interruption in the sheath known as the Node of Ranvier. To bridge this nerve gap, the axon secretes acetylcholine, which acts as a conductor for the impulse.

When any action is repeated over a long period of time, the area of the nerve gap soon becomes saturated with acetylcholine by virtue of the repeated signal impulse. When this occurs, the reaction time for that impulse becomes shortened. Therefore, when one practices the same action over and over, he not only trains the body to perform that action, but also increases the speed with which that action may be performed. Thus, the body is "programmed." Further, after a certain amount of practice, the mind becomes bored with any repetitive action and begins to wander. But the body continues. At this point the mind will begin to dwell on the subtleties of the action or will be so bored that the practice will cease. This is the basis for the adage: "At first a punch is just a punch, but after one thousand punches, a punch is more than a punch, and after ten thousand punches, a punch again becomes just a punch."

The application of Dim Ching relies on striking a specific nerve in such a way as to prevent the impulses from passing a certain point, or to cause the impulses to pass at a faster rate than is normal.

This is generally accomplished by striking certain ganglia of the body, notably those where many nerve bundles converge. The most vulnerable target area of this sort is the vagus nerve. It is particularly susceptible to Dim Ching methods.

Chart B illustrates the physical location of the vagus nerve, which actually controls the action of the heart. The nerves as they descend from the brain are numbered consecutively. The pneumogastric nerve (of which the vagus is a portion) is the tenth nerve and is vulnerable at two points on the neck.

The upper point is located beneath the ear on either side of the head, forward of the mastoid process and just behind the lower rear corner of the mandible. By placing the index finger below the ear, these two protruberances of bone are easily distinguished. The large muscle which runs almost vertically down the side of the neck is the sterno-clieo-mastoideus muscle, and

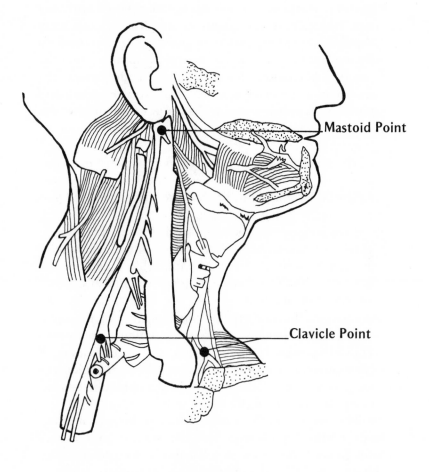

CHART B
Dim Ching Points of the vagus nerve

along the forward edge of this, lies the carotid sheath.

By striking upward onto this point with the Needle Finger (see "Hidden Hand System") with the proper amount of force, the nerve can be traumatized sufficiently to prevent nerve impulses from reaching the heart, while leaving virtually no trace of the attack. Naturally, should you strike too hard, an obvious bruise may result.

Since the body is full of redundant systems, attacking only one of the two vagus nerves seldom produces instant death, though heart failure generally results in three to five days.

Jujitsuka from ancient times have employed pressure to this site with a variety of strangleholds. Usually this takes the form of a cross-collar choke with the knuckle of the thumb being brought to bear against the point with a steady pressure. This, too, prevents the impulse from reaching the heart, causing it to slow down and making the enemy groggy in eight to ten seconds. When the choking pressure is released, the brain again directs the heart to function and the enemy revives. By continuing the pressure long enough, the heart can thus be made to stop without producing any trauma. Depending on the degree of skill of the practitioner, death may result in from two to five minutes.

In contrast, by striking the lower target on the vagus nerve, which lies in the hollow of the neck just inside the frontal tendon of the throat near the proximal fossa of the clavicle, in a downward direction, the pace of the heart may be quickened, inducing ventricular fibrillation. Locate this point by placing the index finger on the corner of the collarbone near the jugular notch. Feel the tendon which joins the notch at this point. Press in slightly downward with the finger and just behind the clavicle lies the nerve. When this attack is performed, the nerve only is traumatized. But since the strike is *toward the distal portion* of the nerve, the brain reacts by sending a stronger signal in the mistaken belief that the heart is not being stimulated. This makes the heart beat much faster than normal, causing a heart attack if executed precisely.

DIM HSUEH
Blood Gate Method

Dim Hsueh, the second realm of Death Touch knowledge, is dependent upon the manipulation of the blood vessels and blood gates. Normally, a ninja taking advantage of Dim Hsueh would induce a heart attack in an enemy by attacking specific points of the body. Death may be delayed through variations in time and pressure.

To comprehend this facet of the Ninja Death Touch, an understanding of the body's circulatory system is necessary. For this reason the following brief lesson in human physiology is offered.

The vital functions of the body depend on the continuous movement of blood through the circulatory system, which is composed of arteries to supply freshly oxygenated blood to the organs and muscles, and the venous system by which expended gases and waste products are removed from the body. The primary motive factor for circulation is the heart. Blood is pumped by the right side of this organ through the pulmonary artery into the lungs where it absorbs oxygen. It then returns through the pulmonary veins to the left side of the heart to be pumped through the aorta and into the arterial system. The red corpuscles supply oxygen to all tissue in the body, and the deoxygenated blood returns through the veins to once again enter the right side of the heart.

The heart is a double-sided pump with four chambers. Valves within these chambers insure the proper direction of blood flow in the circulatory system. These valves are essentially flaps which allow the blood to flow past by flattening against the walls of the arteries. When the flow of blood is reversed (as when the heart is between beats), the back pressure of the blood stands the valves up, closing the channel and preventing the blood from flowing back upon itself.

These valves are found not only in the heart itself, but also throughout the entire circulatory system. In Chinese medicine, they are known as *Hsueh Men,* or "Blood Gates."

The heart muscle receives its oxygen supply from the right and left coronary arteries. Like any muscle, it begins to tire quickly when the flow of blood and oxygen are deprived. Chart C illustrates the location of these arteries. Remember that the heart is merely a specialized muscle, about the size of the two hands cupped together, which lies slightly to the left of the centerline of the body. As can be readily seen from the diagram, the right coronary artery is almost behind the sternum and is therefore not easily accessible. The left coronary artery, however, lies to the left of the sternum, and being exposed as it is on the surface of the organ, is somewhat more vulnerable. This point is shown on Chart C as well.

No two bodies on the Earth are exactly alike, therefore no exact location for this target can be easily determined. Locate the left nipple and extend an imaginary line horizontally across the chest to the right nipple. Next, locate the sternum and the attachments of the ribs on the left side. Between the fifth and sixth ribs, one inch to the left of the sternum, lies the target area.

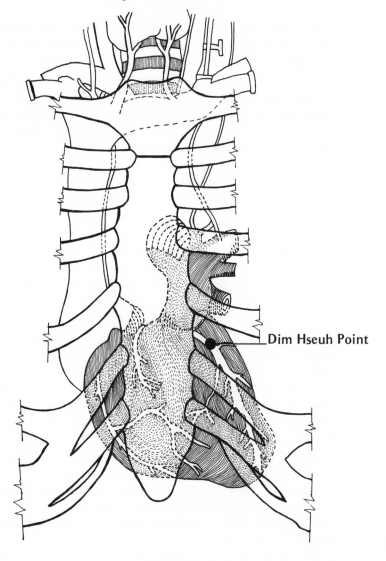

Dim Hseuh Point

CHART C
Dim Hseuh point of the left coronary artery.

It is appropriate at this point to illustrate the inter-action between these circulatory functions and an actual Dim Hsueh strike. The fatal point used here is shown on Chart C. Because a direct relationship exists between the breathing cycle and the valve actions, the strike must be accomplished as the victim exhales, filling the arteries with blood. Employ the Needle Finger for this attack. To multiply its effect, strike at the Hour of the Dragon (11 A.M. to 1 P.M.).

The actual mechanics of this strike require that the artery be flattened onto itself, squeezing the blood out both sides of the artery simultaneously and caus-ing sufficient damage to the arterial valves that blood will no longer flow past the site of the injury. This is not as difficult as it sounds when it is remembered that years of high cholesterol diets, hypertension, and smoking gradually build deposits on the inside of the veins and arteries, clogging and thus narrowing them.

By this method, the Blood Gates (or valves) of the left coronary artery will be sufficiently damaged to halt the flow of blood to the left ventricle. Blood from the venous system enters the heart through the right atrium, passes into the right ventricle, and is pumped along the pulmonary artery into the lungs. Blood returns from the lungs through the pulmonary veins into the left atrium, passes into the left ventricle and is forced out through the aorta into the arteries.

When the left ventricle does not receive sufficient oxygen through the left coronary artery due to the Dim Hsueh strike, it begins to tire and weaken. This leads to an oxygen deficiency in the rest of the body as well. Eventually the heart will cease to function un-less the flow of blood can be restored. This phenome-non is known as cardiac arrest and results in the death of the intended victim.

It should be apparent by this time that the direction of the strike has a great deal to do with the resulting effect on the system. This is true not only as it pertains to blood vessels and nerves, but also in the next section where the flow of Chi is disrupted. In Chinese medicine it may be generally stated that energy directed *against* the normal flow will "sedate" the organ, while energy directed *with the flow* will "tonify" the organ. From this we can see it is a relatively simple matter to overstimulate or starve a given portion of the body by proper striking.

DIM MAK
Chi Flow Method

Chi is the universal life force which flows from, with, and through all things. It is the great river of the Way. When one opposes this flow, one comes into conflict with nature, which seeks only to maintain the balance of the Five Elements.

In Dim Mak, the flow of Chi within the body is altered by manipulation of the meridians. This technique obeys the basic principles of Yin and Yang in that those used to stimulate a given point act to increase the Yang (positive) flow, require that the point be "needled" on the exhalation; that the energy directed to the point be clockwise in nature; and that the strike be made in the direction of the normal flow. Those which are Yin (negative) in origin must inhibit the flow of energy from one point to another; must be performed on the inhalation using counterclockwise energy; and must be directed against the flow.

The Alarm Points shown on Chart D are twelve spots located on the ventral surface of the chest which become spontaneously tender when an illness occurs in the corresponding organ. These points are so clearly

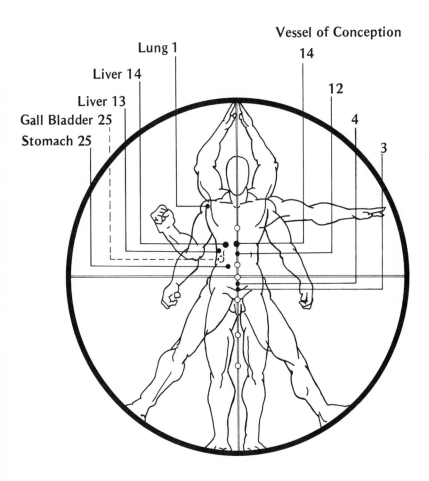

CHART D
Physiological locations of the Points of Alarm.

related to their respective organs that many physicians employ a palpitory method of diagnosis to determine which organ is diseased. These points also serve quite well as points of tonification and sedation in acupuncture, and likewise in Dim Mak.

Any of these alarm points may be attacked with the Needle Finger, bearing in mind the laws of the Death Touch discussed in chapter four.

Time delays in the demise of the victim may be calibrated as follows:

- To strike with heavy pressure will cause an immediate effect.
- To strike with moderate pressure will produce an effect in three days.
- To strike with light pressure causes an effect in one month.
- To strike with no pressure (but merely by the direction of Chi) kills in one year.

It should also be noted that attacks of the first type leave a small bruise at the site of the strike; the second method leaves a small red spot which fades in three to five hours; while the last two leave no trace.

3. INNER STRENGTH

There are two kinds of strength: the outer, which is apparent and fades with age; and the inner, which flows from and through and with all things. It is the latter which is the goal of the ninja.

That the blood, lymph fluids, and nerve impulses circulate within the body is obvious. Much more subtle is the flow of Chi. In Yoga it is said that *prana* (the life force) is contained in the air, and that this energy may be accumulated through meditation. This is true, but even if one never learns Yoga, the body will still absorb this force.

The Chinese believe that all things are descended from *Tao* (the Absolute). That they (the "ten thousand things") are then divided into their positive and negative elements: Yin and Yang. These are then characterized by the Five Elements: Air, Water, Earth, Fire, and Wood. Further, that all things are possessed of Chi, and that ingestion of each increases or decreases the energy to specific areas of the body. In Chinese medicine it is said, "There is only one disease: ingestion; and only one cure: circulation."

This is relevant to the study of Dim Mak in several respects. First because impeding the flow of Chi in the enemy's body will result in illness or death; and second, because to effect this, one must control his own

Chi, by forging the Inner Strength. To accomplish this, one must practice the *Kiai*, or Spirit Shout.

The Kiai is a belly shout, being drawn from the *Hara* (see Chart A). The easiest way to demonstrate this is to assume the classical horse stance and place the fingertips lightly on the lower abdomen. Inhale deeply, filling the lungs from bottom to top. Exhale forcefully, pushing the air from the lungs with the Hara while shouting the word, "who." This will tense the body and expel the air from the lungs while tightening the Hara. You should feel the abdominal wall tense with the fingertips. This is not a scream, drawn from the throat, but more of a grunt. Should you perform it improperly, the voice will become raspy and the throat sore after a few repetitions. Worse still, improper Kiai will rupture the smaller blood vessels of the neck and face.

The purpose of the Kiai is two-fold. First, in combat, the sudden commanding voice will often freeze the enemy, allowing a second or so in which to strike. Second, the Kiai must be delivered from the Hara to establish the flow of Chi to the palm.

Consider the following: every action of the human body is a function of nerve impulse. The brain must consider the action, then direct the muscles to move. Impulses traveling from the brain enter the spinal cord, select the proper "trunk line," and move on toward the muscles to be used.

At the junction of the spinal nerve synapse and the peripheral trunk line to a specific muscle, there exists a small gap. When the nerve impulse reaches this gap, acetylcholine is secreted, bridging the gap to the peripheral nerve. This occurs every time the impulse is sent. Logically, if the same action is repeated several hundred times, this nerve gap will soon become saturated with acetylcholine. This will reduce the reaction time for that specific movement by a considerable degree, as well as help perfect the technique.

Next, consider the adrenal glands, located atop the kidneys. Nature has provided in these a basic survival mechanism. It is known as the *flight-or-fight* reaction. When panic grips the mind, the adrenal glands secrete the powerful stimulant known as adrenaline. This endows one with heightened powers of quickness and almost double one's normal strength.

The function of the Kiai then, is to unite these two physiochemical reactions into a single action, thus multiplying the effect. And, since the muscles of the lower abdominal wall are used to push the air from the lungs, the Chi of the body, having been collected in the Hara, is likewise transmitted.

Kiai, and the secret of mastering your own Chi flow, is the true key to Inner Strength. All Death Touch techniques depend on it.

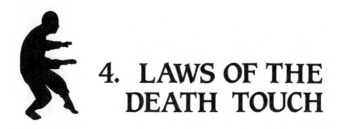

4. LAWS OF THE DEATH TOUCH

The following charts and timetables form the more esoteric laws of the Ninja Death Touch. In Oriental cosmology, there are Five Elements (as opposed to the four elements of European alchemy): Air, Water, Earth, Fire, and Wood. The "ten thousand things" of Lao-Tsu may all be placed into one of these divisions. Then, by understanding the basic principles of interaction, it is possible to predict the outcome of a given situation; or to manipulate that outcome; or merely to observe the outcome and confirm the immutability of Fate.

To hypothetically illustrate the influence of these laws on the Death Touch in modern society, assume that the assigned victim is a middle-aged male with a chronic smoker's cough, in a stressful occupation, who exercises little. Though he does not know it, he has experienced a mild cardiac arhythmia within the last two years. From this description we may assume that the victim will have an accelerated heartbeat (from smoking); high blood pressure (from stress and lack of exercise); and will not be able to defend himself as well as a younger enemy. There are also several psychological angles that go along with such a deteriorated physical state that may be taken advantage of.

The skilled ninja could afflict this man with a stroke, respiratory arrest, or a heart attack. The last of these is the simplest, in this case, and would also be the least suspicious. To appreciate this conclusion, you must understand the laws of the Death Touch.

Chart E shows that the heart is a solid (Yang) organ representing the Fire element. This relationship is also seen in Chart G, which illustrates the relationship of the pulses.

The following Law of the Five Elements states that "Water Destroys Fire" in the Yin (negative) cycle of energy. This is shown on Chart F. We now have the most effective method of inducing the heart attack. We attack the kidneys.

Chart H shows that the Water element is at its peak energy around 5:00 P.M., and that the Fire element will not begin its part of the Chi cycle until 7:00 P.M. Remember also that if the victim has not eaten, he will be more easily agitated, and that if he has eaten, most of his blood supply will be in the digestive organs rather than the pulmonary system. Either way, the heart will not be in a relaxed state.

The Mother-Son Law states that the heart is the "son" of the liver. Therefore we should also attack the liver to have the maximum effect. By employing the Husband-Wife Law, it will be seen that the heart is the "husband" of the spleen. So we may attack this organ as well. By overstimulating the spleen, we make the "wife" stronger than the "husband."

Bear in mind that these are only the Yang aspects of this attack. If we attack the Yin (empty) Water element organ, we must strike the bladder. Further, we could attack the heart more directly by striking the solar plexus.

There is, however, one way to attack the target in question which requires absolutely no physical contact to induce death. As can be seen, to comprehend how this is possible requires an intimate understanding of the laws of the Death Touch, as well as a precise knowledge of human physiology.

The answer is simple: make the victim so angry that he hyperventilates and makes his own heart fibrillate. This should be easy if you have manipulated his day so that it has been a particularly stressful one, and if it is a hot summer afternoon.

This subtle attack would force the victim to unwittingly produce adrenalin, placing undue stress on his heart and vascular system. Given the victim's medical history, most coroners would rule, "Death by natural causes." Yet this ploy can be executed with *no physical contact.*

FA LU WU YUAN SU
The Law of the Five Elements

Energy flows from one organ to another along five pathways and interacts in the following manner:

YIN CYCLE	YANG CYCLE
Water destroys Fire (by extinguishing)	Fire creates Earth (by making ash)
Air (Metal) destroys Wood (by cutting)	Earth creates Air (Metal) (by releasing gases)
Earth destroys Water (by retention)	Air creates Water (by condensation)
Fire destroys Air (Metal) (by melting)	Water creates Wood (by nourishing)
Wood destroys Earth (by covering)	Wood creates Fire (by burning)

It should be noted that later texts on the elements refer to Air as "Metal." This is not the contradiction it may first appear, since the "Sword" has always represented the "Mind" (Air) in Oriental cultures.

FA LU MU CH'IN ERH TZU
The Mother-Son Law

Each element is the "mother" of the element which follows it along the creative cycle and conversely is the "son" of the element which precedes it (see Chart F). Never act directly upon the organ which is diseased in acupuncture. If an organ is weak, tonify its mother. If it is too full, empty (sedate) its son.

Relating this to what we have discussed thusfar, to draw off energy from the heart, one would attack the spleen. To overstimulate the heart, attack the liver.

Chinese scholars long ago categorized all things according to their characteristics as being representative of one of the five elemental states of matter.

The organs themselves are paired in this classification as being of two types: solid and empty.

ELEMENT	SOLID ORGAN	EMPTY ORGAN
Earth	Spleen	Stomach
Water	Kidneys	Bladder
Air	Lungs	Large Intestine
Fire	Heart	Small Intestine
Wood	Liver	Gall Bladder

CHART E
Elemental Relationships of the Organs

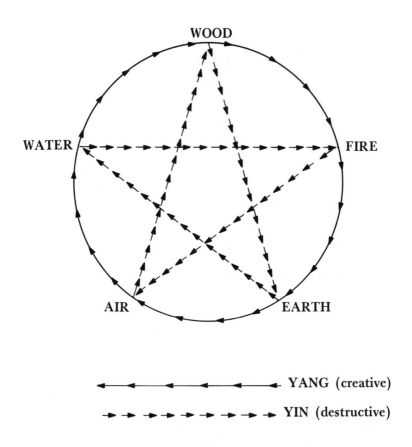

CHART F
Diagrammatical representation of the Yin (destructive)
and Yang (creative) cycles of the Five Elements.

FA LU CHANG FU CH'I TZU
The Husband-Wife Law

Each element is the "husband" of the element it precedes along the Yin (destructive) Cycle and conversely is the "wife" of the element which it follows (see Chart F). The ancient texts of acupuncture state that, "When the husband is strong and the wife is weak, then there is security; when the wife is strong and the husband weak, then there is destruction."

For example, when the heart is deprived of its normal circulation of Chi, the energy flows along the Yin pathway to the lungs, causing congestion.

This relationship is illustrated in the body by the juxtaposition of the twelve pulses. These will not be detailed here since they are primarily medicinal in nature. Chart G lists the elements and the corresponding organ pairs.

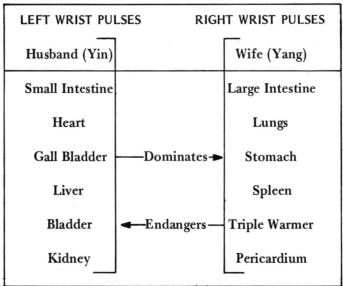

LEFT WRIST PULSES		RIGHT WRIST PULSES
Husband (Yin)		Wife (Yang)
Small Intestine		Large Intestine
Heart		Lungs
Gall Bladder	——Dominates➔	Stomach
Liver		Spleen
Bladder	◄——Endangers——	Triple Warmer
Kidney		Pericardium

CHART G
Elemental relationships of the Husband-Wife Law.

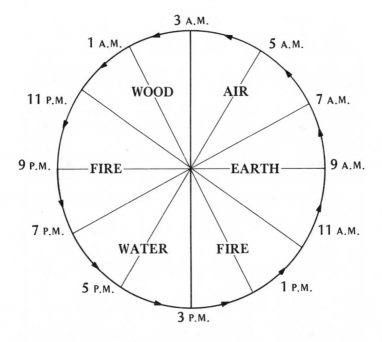

CHART H
Temporal relationships of the Five Elements

The Chinese, in their search for a simple classification system, have named the hours of the day to correspond to the astrological progress of the years. In turn, these also correspond with given organs and elements. The ancient Chinese calender was composed of twelve lunar months consisting of twenty-eight days each. Likewise, the day is divided into twelve hours. The cycle of Chi within the body begins at 3:00 A.M.

Hour Symbol	Time	Organ	Element
Rat	3 A.M.–5 A.M.	Lung	Air (Metal)
Bull (Ox)	5 A.M.–7 A.M.	Large Intestine	Air
Tiger	7 A.M.–9 A.M.	Stomach	Earth
Cat	9 A.M.–11 A.M.	Spleen	Earth
Dragon	11 A.M.–1 P.M.	Heart	Fire
Snake	1 P.M.–3 P.M.	Small Intestine	Fire
Horse	3 P.M.–5 P.M.	Bladder	Water
Goat	5 P.M.–7 P.M.	Kidney	Water
Monkey	7 P.M.–9 P.M.	Pericardium	Fire
Cock	9 P.M.–11 P.M.	Triple Warmer	Fire
Dog	11 P.M.–1 A.M.	Gall Bladder	Wood
Pig	1 A.M.–3 A.M.	Liver	Wood

CHART I
Astrological relationships of the elements and organs.

FA LU CHENG WU-WU YEH
The Midday-Midnight Law

During certain times of the day, the energies transmitted by the Five Elements are more active, due to their natures. At these times, the organs represented by the Five Elements respond more readily to stimuli. The cycle shown on Chart H represents the temporal/energy relationships of the Five Elements. It begins during the middle of the Wood activity period, or at midday, and is half-completed during the second period of Fire activity, or at midnight. This cycle then proceeds through the Earth and Air periods, to begin anew at midday when the old cycle is completed and a new one begins.

Knowledge of the Midday-Midnight Law must be precisely integrated with other information contained in this chapter to be fully comprehended.

5. HIDDEN HAND SYSTEM

The student of the Ninja Death Touch, having completed his studies in its origin, Three Ways, Inner Strength, and laws of the Death Touch, now undertakes the study of the Hidden Hand System. Here is truly the heart of the manipulative function of the Death Touch. It is through this system, as perfected by the Black Dragon Tong of Retribution, that the body's vital and fatal points are attacked.

Because Ninjitsu itself is based on the secrets of invisibility, so is the Hidden Hand System based on the invisibility of the fist in combat. Hence the term, "Hidden Hand."

Encompassed within this general system are the Nine Hand Forms. These are *Ch'ien Ch'uan* (Fore Fist), *Tsai Ch'uan* (Back Fist), *Ch'ui Ch'uan* (Hammer Fist), *Chang Ken* (Palm Heel), *Pien Chang* (Side Palm), *Hsi Chang* (Sucking Palm), *Tao Shou* (Sword Hand), *Mao Shou* (Spear Hand), and *Chen Chih* (Needle Finger). Students of other martial arts will recognize that some of these hand configurations are common to other fighting styles as well. For example, the Ch'ien Ch'uan is similar to the Reverse Punch of Shotokan Karate. Similarly, the Tao Shou of Black Dragon Ninjitsu brings to mind the karateka's classical Shuto. Such similarities in style are not surprising when one considers that many martial forms

41

have a common ancestral form—the exact origin of which has been lost to the mists of time.

The Nine Hand Forms which compose the Hidden Hand System may be divided into three basic types: 1) strikes which employ the various muscles of the hand; 2) strikes which rely on the knuckles for impact; and 3) specialized blows delivered exclusively by the fingertips.

HIDDEN HAND TECHNIQUE

Ninjitsu is an art which is based on invisibility. Not only the invisibility of the individuals who practice the style, but also the invisibility of the fist in combat. Most of the hand weapons in the Hidden Hand System require some flexing of the muscles of the hand to form the proper configuration. An enemy familiar with a given fist style, upon seeing the ninja shape his hand, might deduce the intended target of an attack. To prevent this, and to secure a position near enough to the enemy to strike him, adopt the following Hidden Hand technique.

Turn the left side of the body directly toward the enemy. Aim your left shoulder directly at him. Place the feet in a parallel position, toes pointing straight ahead, in a firm horse stance with your own line of balance perpendicular to that of the enemy. Lower the Hara (see Chart A) slightly for better balance. With your chin tucked against your body for protection, look over your left shoulder directly into the eyes of the enemy. This will help to fix his attention.

Form the weapon by appropriately flexing the muscles of the right hand. Round your shoulders slightly and place this weapon squarely on your Hara. Cover the right fist with the left open hand, concealing the hand weapon.

This stance narrows the target area of the enemy to only your left side. The stance is strong and limits your vulnerability to a circular attack.

Sweep the left hand out in a circular, counterclockwise movement. This action first blocks any left hand attack by the enemy; then continues across the enemy's face, raking his eyes with the back of the extended fingertips; and finally crosses the enemy centerline to deflect any right hand attack which might be thrown in defense.

Simultaneously, the right Hidden Hand seeks out the intended target with the appropriate fist attack. As the right hand strikes, the left drops once again downward across the enemy centerline. If the enemy has raised his arms, or launched an attack, this action of whipping the arm back into play may be used to trap the enemy's arms against his chest. If he has not reacted quickly enough, the left forearm may be used to seize his jacket and pull him into the blow.

This method is actually quite simple, but is difficult at first to the untrained. It is performed at close quarters with the body turned slightly away from the enemy to control his area of attack.

CH'IEN CH'UAN
Fore Fist

The cornerstone of the Hidden Hand System is the Ch'ien Ch'uan, or Fore Fist, first of the Nine Hand Forms.

Make this hand weapon by first curling the fingers into the palm, beginning with the little finger. Tuck the fingertips into the hand so that they are held in place by the mount of venus at the base of the thumb. Bend the thumb at the knuckle and place the ball of the thumb on top of the fingers, pressing downward

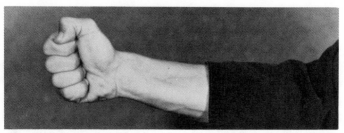

Figure 1

to lock the fingers together (figure one).

In Occidental boxing, the thumb is placed *over* the fingers. As many karateka have found, however, this position sometimes allows the thumb to become entangled in the uniform of the enemy.

As an example, one of the most devastating applications here is the Fore Fist to chin strike. Having cocked the fist on your hip, strike out with a twisting punch, striking the enemy squarely on the point of the chin. The impact need be no more than that used in striking any other target; i.e., eight pounds. The effectiveness of this blow is derived from the action of snapping the head back and jarring the brain, thus stunning the enemy, rather than any tissue damage that may be done to the face (figure two).

For the next example application of the Fore Fist, refer to symbol ⊜ on Chart A, and locate the xyphoid process. This is a small, sword-shaped bone attached to the end of the sternum by a cartilage hinge.

By striking this point with the Fore Fist, the phrenic nerve which controls the respiratory action of the diaphragm may be traumatized (figure three). The result of a proper blow to this point is that the enemy will be "unable to catch his breath." The diaphragm will cease to pump air into and out of the lungs because it receives no nerve impulse from the brain instructing it to do so.

The enemy may lapse into unconsciousness in ninety seconds or so from lack of oxygen. When this occurs, the body will begin to breath autonomously, using the muscles along the rib cage. This will prevent death and eventually revive the victim.

Should the blow be delivered with heavy force, the phrenic nerve will be permanently damaged. In this event, the victim will not revive spontaneously, but will

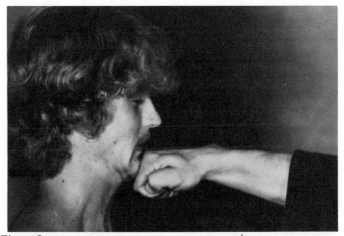

Figure 2

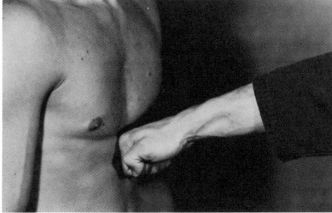

Figure 3

require artificial respiration if death is to be prevented.

In its most severe application, the Fore Fist is used to snap-off the xyphoid process and drive it into the diaphragm. This will sever the phrenic nerve and result in the death of the victim. This, however, leaves a visible wound, and is therefore not the true Death Touch.

TSAI CH'UAN
Back Fist

Just as the point of the first two knuckles are the striking surface in the Fore Fist, the backs of these may also be employed to strike the enemy. This is known as the Tsai Ch'uan, or Back Fist. It is performed by loading the fist on the opposite hip, lifting the elbow, and snapping out with the back of the hand to the enemy's temple. At this site, the bones of the skull are sufficiently weak and thin so that even a relatively mild blow can have a devastating effect. Additionally, the temporal blood vessels may be easily ruptured, inducing unconsciousness and death (figure four).

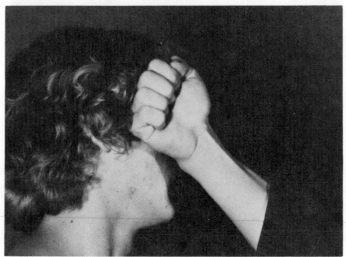

Figure 4

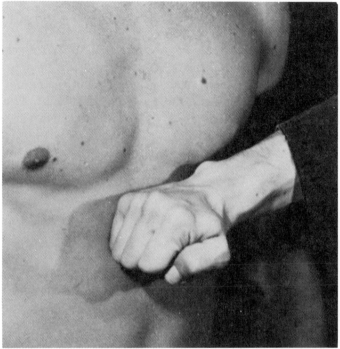

Figure 5

CH'UI CH'UAN
Hammer Fist

Yet another form within the Hidden Hand System is called the Ch'ui Ch'uan, or Hammer Fist. Here the muscles on the little finger side of the hand are used to strike the target, in this example, the solar plexus. This attack will have a similar effect to that shown in figure three, and may be directed alternately against the diaphragm. The arm should exert the same snapping motion common to the other fist strikes (figure five).

CHANG KEN
Palm Heel

This technique is known as Chang Ken, or Palm Heel. The striking surface is the heel of the hand as formed by the base of the mount of mars muscle, and the mount of venus (which lies at the base of the thumb). The action of the strike is always from the shoulder, since this adds one's body weight to the impact of the blow.

Form the fist by curling the fingers slightly into the hand to tense the muscles indicated above. Bend the wrist back so that the heel of the hand lies directly in front of the end of the wrist. Bend the thumb to add to this isometric tension. Strike with the same action as is employed in the Fore Fist.

Once contact has been made by this hand weapon, the fingers may be used to seize the enemy uniform or muscles. If the punch is directed against the face, the fingers may be employed to gouge the eyes, rip the cheeks, or even secure a hold on the enemy by gripping the jawbone through the skin.

The simplest attack with the Palm Heel is the chin strike. Practice this technique by holding your left palm face down in front of your face at chin level. Strike upward into the left palm with the right Palm Heel.

When directed against the chin of the enemy, this action drives the head straight up and back, jamming the base of the skull against the medulla. Also the cervical vertebrae are pinched together, inducing a whiplash-type concussion (figure six).

PIEN CHANG
Side Palm

A variation of this hand form is the Side Palm, known also as Pien Chang. The Side Palm is a particularly effec-

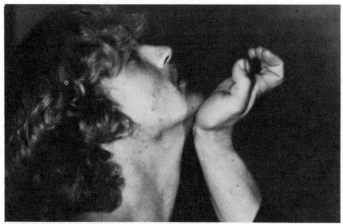

Figure 6

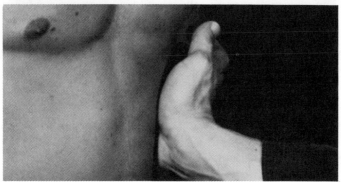

Figure 7

tive means of delivering certain Death Touch blows to the body. For example, figure seven illustrates a Side Palm executing a spleen punch. Note that the heel of the hand strikes the point of the lowest rib on the enemy's left side. Results will be either to snap off the tip of the rib, driving it into the spleen, or to draw out the energy of the Earth elements through the Alarm Point located at this site. The latter technique only is part of the Ninja Death Touch philosophy and approach, since the former will leave a bruise at the very least.

HSI CHANG
Sucking Palm

The sixth of the Nine Hand Forms, Hsi Chang (Sucking Palm), is singularly effective when attacking the heart. The hand is shaped into a looser, more open version of the Palm Heel, the point of impact being the heel of the hand (figure eight). The form relies not so much on its physical nature as it does on the ninja's capacity to induce his own Chi flow into the Sucking Palm. A specific application is called for here, as is shown by the following illustration.

Begin the technique by loading the hand, fingers down, palm turned toward the enemy, on the near hip. The elbow is *behind* the shoulder, forming a ninety degree angle. The force of the strike is derived from the Hara. Chi must flow from this site, up the torso, into the shoulder, and finally to the valley of the moon, which lies in the "V" of the palm between the mounts of mars and venus.

During training, this area should "tingle" as it becomes charged with the negative (Yin) energy necessary to kill. This sensation is the basis for legends of a "red glow" about the hands of the ancient masters.

The strike is effected by bringing the fist, fingers down, to the centerline of the body in front of the Hara. Then continue driving upward at a forty-five degree angle, simultaneously turning the fingers uppermost, to hit the *Hua Kai Hsueh,* or "Blood Gate of the Open Lotus." This is located two finger widths above the xyphoid process in a slight depression of the sternum proper.

The impact must be such that the sternum is compressed by the hand over the entire surface of the palm heel, to "squeeze" the heart. It is best to deliver the blow just before the heart beats, as it fills with blood.

If this is not possible, strike as the target prepares to exhale. This action disrupts the rhythm of the heart, making it beat before it is ready. Since the organ is filled with blood, rupture of the heart itself is possible, if enough force is employed. Proper striking, however, leaves no mark.

The blow thus induces cardiac arhythmia and ventricular fibrillation, causing death by apparent heart attack. The concept of the masters in this case was to draw the energy out of the heart with the palm. The strike is not a driving, crushing blow, but rather a pumping action.

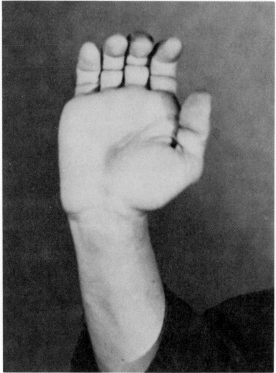

Figure 8

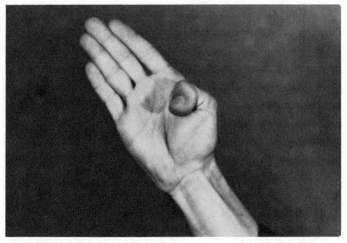

Figure 9

TAO SHOU
Sword Hand

This weapon is formed by extending the fingers together, then flexing the fingers upward as if trying to lift all four toward the thumb side of the hand. This action tenses the muscle which lies along the outside edge of the palm.

Next, the thumb is cocked into the hand by bending at the knuckle. This creates the proper tension in the muscles and locks the fist together (figure nine).

The outside edge of the hand may be used to strike the vital points of the enemy's body. Shown in figure ten is the classical throat application of the Sword Hand.

The first knuckle of the index finger may be used to attack the enemy in a wide hooking-type punch. This method is known as the Ridge Hand in modern karate, and is best employed against targets where blood vessels or nerves lie near the surface, the temple, for example (figure eleven).

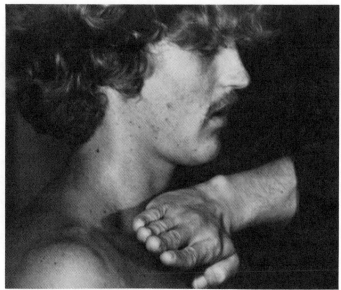

Figure 10

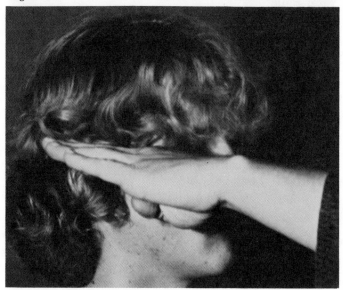

Figure 11

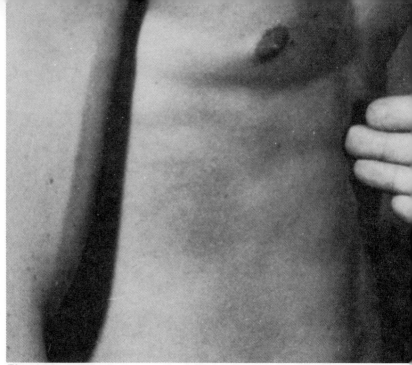

Figure 12

MAO SHOU
Spear Hand

Mao Shou, or the Spear Hand, is the eighth of the
Nine Hand Forms. It is certainly one of the most difficult of all the forms to master, requiring a special
training program and years of intense practice to become adept in its use. It resembles the Iron Hand style
common to Southern China, which is characterized by
a fusion of the knuckles, fingers, and metacarpals of the
hand. Yet turning the hand into a nerveless club is
hardly advisable during the present age.

To train for the Spear Hand, obtain a large kettle or
clay pot and fill it with black beans to a depth of eighteen inches.

The Spear Hand is formed exactly as the Sword Hand
is, with the exception that the striking surface is the fingertips rather than the mount of mars. Load the right
Spear Hand with the palm held just under the right arm-
pit, fingers pointing straight down.

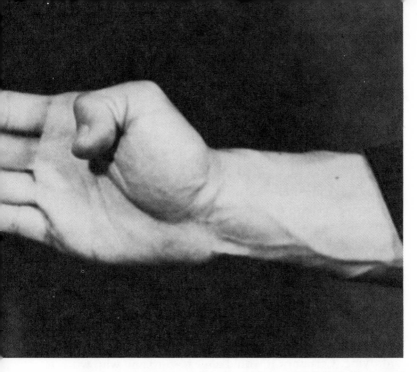

Extend the left hand and lightly touch the center of the training kettle with the tip of the middle finger. This hand is palm down. Now strike downward into the kettle with the right hand, turning the palm over in flight and penetrating as deeply as possible. Repeat this exercise one thousand times. Kiai every fifth punch. Do this each day for one year.

Next, fill the kettle with rice and practice as before for one year. Finally, fill the kettle with pebbles and practice for one year. When you can penetrate through all the stones and touch the bottom of the kettle, you will have mastered the Spear Hand.

With this technique it is actually possible to penetrate an enemy's body by striking the xyphoid process. At this point, the thoracic cavity and the abdominal cavity are divided by the diaphragm, and the musculature and mesentery of the body are at their weakest.

In the Death Touch application, the xyphoid process is struck with the extended fingertips, but no attempt is made to penetrate the body (figure twelve).

The effect is the same as in striking this point with the Fore Fist, except that the Spear Hand allows for more precision of application.

Black Dragon Sensei also supplemented their practice by juggling iron balls to counteract, in part, the destructive effect which kettle practice has on the hands.

There is a legend among martial artists that a ninja could pull out his enemy's heart and show it to him before he died. Considering the awesome power of the Spear Hand. this legend is no doubt based on fact. Such an attack would not only be stunning in the extreme, but also produce immediate shock. It is possible that the victim could see his own heart before collapsing and dying. Certainly it would appear so to any who witnessed such an event.

CHEN CHIH
Needle Finger

Chen Chih, or Needle Finger, is the last of the Nine Hand Forms encompassed within the Hidden Hand System. It is the final hand weapon to be discussed because it relies on *only one finger* to inflict damage, but requires years of kettle practice to attain true mastery.

The Needle Finger is formed by extending the fingertips, then curling the middle, ring, and little fingers into the palm slightly so that they form a base upon which the index finger may rest while pointing forward. The thumb is extended along the index finger at the lower portion with the side of the thumb pressing against base (figure thirteen).

The index finger should be held straight but not locked rigid. This can lead to a broken finger. Also, the nail must be trimmed short to prevent it from splitting on impact.

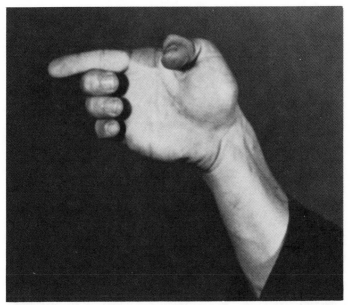

Figure 13

The Needle Finger may be directed against any of the vital or fatal points of the body. For instance, one excellent target is the Mastoid Point, which lies along the side of the neck (see Chart B). By striking this bundle of blood vessels and nerves which flow through the carotid sheath to the body, it is possible to induce a severe nerve trauma and bleeding. A lighter strike applied as the enemy exhales and the carotid artery is filled with blood will create blood clots, which will be carried to the brain, causing an embolism (figure fourteen).

A secondary, and more difficult application, is the Dim Hsueh point of the coronary artery shown on Chart C. To effect this strike, one must slip the Needle Finger between the ribs of the enemy to attack this small artery, which supplies blood to the heart itself. The enemy will soon develop a heart condition and expire (figure fifteen).

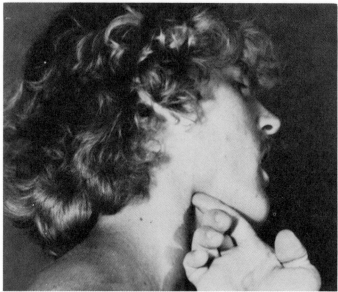

Figure 14

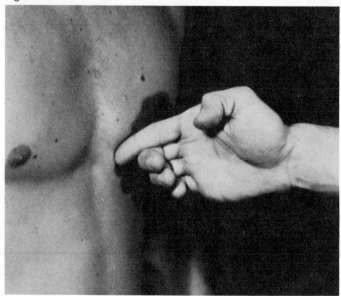

Figure 15

TUAN T'IEH CH'UAN
Forging the Fist

After the student has completed study of the Hidden Hand System, he must undertake the mastery of the strike motion itself. Through this means are the hand weapons brought into contact with the body's various vital and fatal points.

First of the Nine Hand Forms, the Fore Fist, is the most commonly used by practicing ninja. It is truly the cornerstone of the Hidden Hand System. To attain its mastery requires devotion to a special training program, one which centers on the development of Chi flow, the basics of which follow. Master the Fore Fist and combat application of the remaining eight Hand Forms will come naturally.

To practice the Fore Fist, one must first construct a striking post. Select a wooden post as tall as you are and as big around as the thickest portion of your thigh. Set the post into the earth deeply enough so that the top is just above solar plexus level. Secure a length of rope to the top of the post and wrap it around the circumference enough times to cover the post down to waist level. Secure the end of the rope to the post at this point. The rope used should be at least one inch thick, since it will be the only padding between your hand and the wood beneath.

After constructing a striking post, Fore Fist training may begin. Rise early in the morning, before dawn if possible, to begin practice. Face the East and assume a horse stance one arm's length from the striking post. Focus your attention on the center of the post at solar plexus level. (Note: This will now be halfway between the top and the bottom of the wrapped section, since the proper stance lowers the Hara.) Load the right Fore

Fist on the right hip, knuckles uppermost. Extend the left hand and turn the palm out. The fingernails of the left hand should be lightly touching the side of the target at the proper level. The purpose of the left hand in this technique is two-fold. First, it is used to measure the target's distance, increasing accuracy. Second, in actual combat, the lapel of the enemy may be seized by the left hand and employed to pull him into the blow.

The points of the first two knuckles are the striking surface of this fist. Execute the technique by bringing the right hand to the centerline of the body and driving straight to the target. Simultaneously, pull the left hand to the left hip, forming a second loaded Fore Fist. The need for this action is based on a law of physics: "For every action, there must be an equal and opposite reaction." Further, it adds impact to the right fist and prevents the body from becoming unbalanced.

Note that the wrist is turned over as the punch travels to the target. This imparts "snap" to the fist. Note also that the shoulder is not thrown into the punch, but rather is held in its original position: square and facing the target.

Now reset, and strike with the left fist in a similar manner. This completes one cycle. Repeat one thousand times per day for one year. Kiai every fifth punch. This will tighten the Hara and prepare the Yin Yu Channels of the arm for the flow of Chi.

Gradually you will beat the rope flat with your knuckles. Do not replace the padding, but continue to strike as before. This will toughen the wrist and the knuckles. Some schools advocate smashing the first two knuckles and allowing the cartilage to fuse the bones together. This produces an unnecessary deformity. Control is the object of this training, not pain.

Do not hit the striking post until you are in great pain. Rather, strike lightly and let the constant practice develop the blow properly. After a time, the punch will rebound effortlessly on impact. This is what you seek, the "snapping" punch.

TAMESHIWARA
Breaking Test

Select a white pine board one foot square with a thickness of one inch, free of knots and cross grain. Secure this with the grain horizontal and the center of the board at solar plexus level. Prepare as before and strike the center in a slightly downward motion in the center with the Fore Fist.

Eight pounds of pressure are required to break the board in this manner with no pain. This is proper technique. No more force than this is required to kill with the Ninja Death Touch.

Note that it is sufficient to break one board *with the grain* as a valid test of the Fore Fist. Some may argue that multiple board breaks are a greater test of power. But this is the external power of which they speak, not the true Chi.

6. THE NINE FATAL BLOWS

Before beginning actual training in the application and technique of the Ninja Death Touch, a few words concerning the mechanics of this system are in order. As has been seen until now, the knowledge thus far related is by no means mysterious. Nor does it depend on supernatural powers beyond those of the general martial artist. In point of fact, the majority of this study consists of simple lessons in anatomy and physiology.

There are, however, certain aspects of the human body that defy explanation. For instance, it is a medical fact that a sharp blow to the top of the head will sometimes produce insipidus diabetes in the human. This is true even though there is no medical foundation to support it. The portion of the brain which receives the shock is in no way related to the function of the pancreas. Likewise, no nerves or blood vessels flow from this site to the organ without myriad convolutions in the body. How then, can this phenomenon be explained?

Chinese acupuncture provides a clue. Located at the top of the skull, on the meridian known as the Governing Vessel, lies the twenty-first of thirty points which begin at the base of the spine and end on the upper mandible.

In Chinese medicine, it is this point which controls

the flow of Chi to the pancreas. Here, then, lies the answer. The reader may ask why such a blow does not always induce insipidus diabetes. Not surprisingly, because the blow must be timed to the season, time of day, respiration, and the direction of Chi flow. When one has learned to take these factors into consideration, the technique will be effective each time it is utilized.

THE NINE FATAL BLOWS

Following is a photographically illustrated study of the Nine Fatal Blows of the Dim Mak Way. Each is a specific attack system designed to destroy the respective major organs of the body. These include *Hsin Chuan* (Heart Punch), *Fei Chuan* (Lung Punch), *Shen Chuan* (Kidney Punch), *Hsueh K'u Chuan* (Spleen Punch), *P'ang Kuang Chuan* (Bladder Punch), *Kan Chuan* (Liver Punch), *Te Ch'ang Chuan* (Small Intestine Punch), *Ta Ch'ang Chuan* (Large Intestine Punch), *We Chuan* (Stomach Punch). Calculated into each attack is a time delay feature. This means that total destruction of the organ in question, and ensuing metabolic trauma and failure may be delayed for a week to a year, depending on the skill of the practitioner.

Note that the Ninja Death Touch is a Way of Knowledge, rather than a way of action. For this reason, the reader should understand that the hand weapons within the Hidden Hand System, stances, and strategies (which are generally drawn from the *Kumi-Uchi,* or "Ninja Combat System") may be interchanged, depending on the nature of the terrain, opponent's skill level, time and season, and so on.

In other words, the student must not feel constrained to use only the attack strategies which follow. Be flexible instead. If a particular Hand Form seems appropriate, use it. An instructor can never be replaced by a book, which by its very nature is limited in its capacity to impart information to the student. In such a regard, this work is no different than any other martial arts text.

Remember that each organ represents an element, then follow the destructive cycle of the Five Elements. Then wait.

HSIN CHUAN
Heart Punch

Vessel of Conception Alarm Point Fourteen (see Chart D) is one of the few forbidden points of acupuncture, meaning that it is never to be "needled" or pierced. When using this point medicinally, moxibustion is the preferred method of treatment. This point becomes spontaneously tender in the event of heart diseases. This is especially so of Yang-based illnesses, or those of excess, such as hypertension.

The technique for applying this blow, known as *P'ao*, is essentially a method of moving in on the enemy under his attack and striking the centerline of his body at solar plexus level. In ancient times, this technique was sometimes called *Shan Te Huo Yen* or "Fan the Flame." P'ao represents Fire in the Five Elements, and is a linear Yang action which moves forward. Therefore it will add energy to the heart, making it beat harder, much in the same manner as an automobile with the choke stuck open.

When properly executed, this technique leaves no trace. The hand weapon is the Palm Heel. Strike at the moment of your own exhalation at the same time the victim inhales. This will make his body accept the additional energy you will transmit.

The energy of P'ao is "pounding," as in the sudden firing of a gun. Since it is performed on the exhalation, the technique is accompanied by a Kiai.

Figure 16

Assume the standard three-point stance shown in figure sixteen, with forty percent of your weight on the lead leg and sixty percent on the rear leg. Shoulders must be square to the enemy, hands held vertically in front of the centerline, forming Sword Hands initially.

P'ao works best against a downward striking action, as in an overhead knife attack where the enemy is stabbing downward. In unarmed combat it is best used against the overhead right lead.

As the enemy begins his attack, step diagonally forward and to the left with your left foot beneath his arm, while executing a rising forearm block to halt his punch. This is known as *Stealing the March,* because as the enemy advances, you advance and cut him off. Further, the effect of the Kiai will be to psychologically stun the enemy, breaking his rhythm and blunting his attack in midstride. Simultaneously, strike Vessel of Conception Alarm Point Fourteen with the Palm Heel from slightly below, angling the punch upward forty-five degrees (figure seventeen). This punch alone is sufficient to incapacitate an ordinary man.

Immediately as you strike, draw the right foot near your left ankle into a basic cat stance. As you draw the right side of your body from in front of the collapsing enemy, sweep a large arc clockwise with your right arm. The enemy right arm should be at shoulder level as you pass beneath it. When you have cleared the enemy and assumed the cat stance beside him, end the arc of the right arm by placing the right palm on the right shoulder or arm of the enemy. This is known as the *Sleepy Hand Parry,* so named because such gentle pressure is applied. It is as if one were waking a sleeping relative. The purpose of the parry is simply to touch the enemy, allowing you to sense his next movement. In this instance, it will be to fall to the ground (figure eighteen).

Figure 17

Figure 18

FEI CHUAN
Lung Punch

To strike Lung Alarm Point One (see Chart D) requires a more exotic technique. Since the target lies on the upper distal corner of the pectoral muscle, it is not as easily accessible as those on the centerline of the body. The technique is called *Heng,* which means "Crossing." Heng represents Earth among the Five Elements.

From the three-point stance, employ Heng against any straight left lead. As the enemy launches his attack, step straight forward with your left foot, closing the gap between yourself and the enemy (figure nineteen).

Figure 19

Figure 20

Simultaneously execute a palm-up block with your left hand. This action is the same as a shoulder block, except that the hand remains open (figure twenty).

Before the enemy can withdraw his arm from the attack, turn your left hand over counterclockwise and pull down on his forearm slightly. Step quickly forward with the left foot and execute a block with the Fore Fist, first of the Nine Hand Forms. The arc of this action will carry your right fist below the enemy's extended left arm, to his inside line, allowing you to strike Lung Meridian Point One with your right thumb knuckle (figure twenty-one).

In attacking the lungs, remember that the flow of Chi is from the center of the chest (although it is not accessible at that point) toward the hand. When this attack is properly executed, the enemy arm will be numbed for about one hour. This is a sign that you have struck correctly.

The action of this blow is to stifle the flow of Chi from the lungs. The enemy will seldom die right away, but will develop any one of fifteen different illnesses related to congestion of the organ itself (pneumonia, tuberculosis, etcetera) and expire in one year.

That is the beauty of this technique: that the fight can be ended by paralyzing the enemy's arm temporarily, while the actual Death Touch will not even begin to take effect for three months.

Figure 21

SHEN CHUAN
Kidney Punch

To attack the kidneys, one must strike Gall Bladder Alarm Point Twenty-five found on Chart D. Since this point lies on the back, it is necessary to execute a forward-turning pivot to make it accessible. The Kidney Punch, third of the Nine Fatal Blows, is best employed against an attack to the body, especially the straight left to the solar plexus.

From the three-point stance, as the enemy throws his left punch (figure twenty-two), execute a parry by scooping under the enemy's left arm and turning into a side stance. This enables you to evade the punch as well as deflect the attack to the enemy's inside line (figure twenty-three).

Step diagonally forward and to his outside line with your right foot, while maintaining pressure against his elbow with your left hand. Now pivot on the ball of the left foot. Shift your weight over your right leg and slip into the three-point stance once more. You are now behind the left shoulder of the enemy (this is not always a good position to be in, since it could make you vulnerable to a spinning backfist). As you gain this position, strike the enemy with a right Side Palm directed to Gall Bladder Alarm Point Twenty-five, which is located just above the left kidney (figure twenty-four).

The effect of this Death Touch technique is often profound in the extreme. Notably, the sciatic nerve, which lies in the same vicinity, may be injured. In this event, the enemy will drop to his knees, ending the fight.

If the blow is properly executed, the enemy will drop to one knee and lay his hand palm-out over the injury. He will recover from the strike within three days, but

Figure 22

Figure 23

the flow of Chi will once again be disrupted. In this case, renal shutdown will occur within one year. Death is likely to follow.

Figure 24

Figure 25

HSUEH K'U CHUAN
Spleen Punch

The target organ here is the spleen. The weapon is, once again, the Side Palm, in this instance, thrown from the hip.

This technique is best used against a fighter who shows a fondness for quick, left-right, or one-two, punches. Having blocked his attack with a rising forearm block a time or two, gauge his rhythm and timing. As he throws his left jab, step directly to your left with your left foot, into a facing horse stance. Remember, you have previously blocked his combination using a different technique twice; he will anticipate the same action this third time. As you step, execute a left-handed cross block, deflecting his jab to the outside and allowing it to slip past your right ear (figure twenty-five).

Pivot on the heel of the left foot ninety degrees towards your right front, and assume a side stance perpendicular to the enemy line of balance. You should be directly in front of him as he turns into his right cross. Execute a sweeping block with your left hand against his punch, allowing his arm to pass in front of your chest (figure twenty-six). Your right hip is now aimed at his Hara; your right hand is loaded on your hip as you perform the block. Drive your right Side Palm onto his

Figure 26

Figure 27

chest on the left side striking squarely on the tip of the
lowest floating rib (figure twenty-seven). It is possible
to snap off the rib and drive it into the left lung with
this blow, but sufficient pressure need only be exerted
to bend the rib, causing it to stab the diaphragm
slightly. This will end the fight. The long-term effect
will be arteriosclerosis, dysfunction of the immune
systems of the body, and/or splenic collapse within one
year.

Figure 28

Figure 29

P'ANG KUANG CHUAN
Bladder Punch

The next technique, the fifth of the Nine Fatal Blows, is best employed against a low hooking blow to the body. As the enemy steps up with his hook, fade back away from him slightly by shifting your weight over your rear leg. At the same time execute a Serpent Parry with your left hand against his punch. Bring your right hand to your own centerline and load the Needle Finger next to your right pectoral (figure twenty-eight).

Immediately as you have deflected his punch, shift your weight over the lead leg and draw the right foot up to the left ankle into the cat stance. Once again you have stolen the march. From this position the enemy cannot strike you with his left hand for you are inside the arc of his fist. His right hook is expended, and since your legs are together defensively, there is little chance for a knee attack. His best chance is to grapple with you. Before he can do so, you must strike down at a forty-five degree angle, hitting Vessel of Conception Alarm Point Three with the Needle Finger (figure twenty-nine).

This attack not only hits the pressure point, it also attacks the bladder itself and the nerves which lie atop the pubic arch. The enemy will lock his knees together and fall as if he had been struck in the groin. The delayed effect is prostatitus, inflammation of the urethra, and/or thrombosis of the bladder within one year.

KAN CHUAN
Liver Punch

The next of the Nine Fatal Blows, Kan Chuan (Liver Punch), utilizes the Spear Hand to deliver the killing strike. From a basic side stance, step in with the left foot and narrow the gap between yourself and the enemy, while feinting a left Palm Heel to the head (figure thirty). Remember, when attacking the head, you must move one full step, while when attacking the body, you need move only one-half step. This action should cause the enemy to lean slightly back from the jab. Fight with a low lead hand and initiate the previous feint from the wrist.

Figure 30

Figure 31

Now take a following step with your right foot as you drop your left hand from the jab, making it appear that you are merely replacing your guard hand. Actually, you have advanced into within the enemy's arc while he flinched at your jab. Now he will relax for a second, thinking that you are still out of range. If he is not an aggressive fighter, he may blink (figure thirty-one).

Step quickly forward once again with the left foot, inside the enemy lead leg, while ducking low. Form the left hand into the Spear Hand. Using a left hooking strike, hit the enemy at the fatal point located by the second lowest floating rib. This is the site of Liver Alarm Point Fourteen (figure thirty-two).

Sufficient other nerves exist at this site to induce shock to the liver so that unconsciousness from this blow is fairly common in professional boxing. In the Dim Mak application, however, hepatitus is the normal result. While this may not seem like a "death blow" in this day and age, try to recall the relatively primitive state of medicine when these techniques were developed. In that time, jaundice (the classic symptom of liver dysfunction) often meant death within one year.

Kan Chuan is still an efficient and debilitating blow, one which is most useful to have at your disposal.

Figure 32

TE CH'ANG CHUAN
Small Intestine Punch

We shall combine instruction in the seventh of the Nine Fatal Blows with that in a problem peculiar to Death Touch practitioners: the technique needed to deliver a strike to an opponent's *body* at the same time he launches an attack against you. Te Ch'ang Chuan, or Small Intestine Punch, is the blow to be learned in this instance.

Part of the problem with striking an enemy as he attacks has to do with timing. Because the techniques to be used in such instances are composed of several parts, the problem of timing is further compounded. One of the most basic methods of insinuating your strike in spite of the enemy's attack is the shift. The sequence here goes something like this: as the enemy attacks, the ninja falls slightly back, then quickly recovers and delivers a counterstrike. In fencing this sequence is known as the *riposte*.

Begin the exercise by assuming that your opponent has just thrown a straight, right-handed punch at you. Deflect the enemy attack to the middle quarter with a downward thrust of your left forearm. This works best when the enemy does not advance. Point the left toes inward, forming a side stance. Place the right hand near your head for protection (figure thirty-three).

As he draws his arm back, follow him by stepping inside with your left foot, pivoting towards him on the balls of both feet. Form the right hand into an inverted Palm Heel and deliver the blow in the manner of an upper cut to Vessel of Conception Alarm Point Four (figure thirty-four). Bear in mind that the Hara is two inches below the navel, and this point is three.

Since the small intestine is representative of the Fire element, and since the heart is also Fire, being related to

Figure 33

Figure 34

the small intestine in the deep and superficial circulation of energy, whatever affects the small intestine affects the heart. This blow will thus steal the strength of the enemy. The delayed effect will be malnutrition, since the small intestine will be unable to properly digest food thereafter. Colitis is the most common symptom.

TA CH'ANG CHUAN
Large Intestine Punch

The large intestine is represented by Air among the Five Elements, as are the Lungs. Thus, whatever affects one also affects the other. Likewise, the type of attack should be similar.

In the Lung Punch, the technique involved sweeping the weapon hand around to within the enemy's arc to reach the target. This was a circular action revolving about a linear axis. The same principle will be applied to the Large Intestine Punch, also known as Ta Ch'ang Chuan.

Start this eighth Fatal Blow exercise by driving the enemy back by advancing with the lead foot and attacking his eyes with the left Spear Hand. This will induce him to lift his guard and step slightly back with his trailing leg (figure thirty-five).

Figure 35

Figure 36

Trap the enemy lead arm with your left arm and pivot on the heel of the left foot one hundred-eighty degrees to your right rear corner, advancing into the enemy field by spinning about the left leg. As you execute this pivot, bend the knees deeply, lowering your center of gravity and your head. Keep the back straight and the head no higher than the enemy shoulder. Load the right Hammer Fist near your right cheek, and allow the whip of the pivot to swing your fist out horizontally at your own shoulder level. The right fist will strike the ascending portion of the large intestine at the site of Stomach Alarm Point Twenty-five (figure thirty-six). Again, dysfunction of the organ itself is the long-term effect, leading to malnutrition and death within one year.

WEI CHUAN
Stomach Punch

The last of the Nine Fatal Blows, Wei Chuan (Stomach Punch), also requires special closing techniques in order to penetrate the enemy's defensive arc. For this reason another hypothetical fighting scenario has been constructed as follows. The technique is known as Tsuan, and is related to Water among the Five Elements.

The target for attacking the stomach is Vessel of Conception Alarm Point Twelve. It lies on the centerline of the body one hand width below the sternum.

The lesson begins with the ninja's opponent throwing a right hook to the body. Deflect the enemy hook with a left forearm parry, and simultaneously kick out with your left toes. Load your right Fore Fist on your right hip. This attack on the part of the enemy opens his centerline to attack. Further, it forces him to bend over slightly as he throws his punch. If he is a good fighter, he will lower his center of gravity rather than bend in such a manner (figure thirty-seven).

Figure 37

Figure 38

Assuming that he is not an expert fighter and bends as anticipated, pivot on the heel of the left foot one hundred-eighty degrees to your right front corner and strike upward from your right hip with the uppercut Fore Fist, landing the blow squarely on the fatal point (figure thirty-eight). Maintain sufficient downward pressure against the enemy arm to be sure that he leans into the blow. This alone will incapacitate him. The delayed Ninja Death Touch effect will be peptic ulcers (those found where the esophagus joins the upper portion of the stomach). Persons with this condition die within one year unless treatment is forthcoming.

7. POWER OF LIFE AND DEATH

In ancient times, many phenomenal powers were attributed to the masters of Ninjitsu. Notable among these was the power to kill and then restore life. Death Touch practitioners have for centuries tested their technique in this manner. Sometimes the subjects were willing, as in the case of a challenge; sometimes they were not, as with Hideo in "The Unwilling Agent" parable. Occasionally, an outlaw band would confront a local Master seeking to test his skill. In such an event, the leader, or the individual challenger, was "killed" and then restored to life. He would then be given the choice of serving the Master (since such techniques sometimes caused brain damage, resulting in a zombie-like state); leaving the province forever (if the challenger had shown any promise); or returning to the Land of the Dead (in the event he had not learned his lesson).

Used in this demonstration is the Sword Hand. The vital point to be attacked is Lung Alarm Point One, found on Chart D. It is strongly suggested that the student devote no less than ten years' time to the study of Ninjitsu and Death Touch principles before attempting the following exercise. Be warned!

Place the subject facing toward you in a standard horse stance and assume a similar position one arm's length away with the Sword Hand loaded near the right

Figure 39

ear. If the subject has volunteered for this test (as the zealous often do), check the timetables and charts to insure that the time of day is not conducive to causing death. *This is only a test!*

Allow him to relax and breath normally. Measure the blow slowly, without making contact (figure thirty-nine). Make note of whether or not he flinches. If he does, select another volunteer. Watch his breathing, since you must take care to strike on the exhalation. Now using only *half the force required to kill,* apply

Figure 40

the blow. Immediately observe the subject's reaction (figure forty).

His color will pale and he may perspire spontaneously, he may swallow, and his eyes will glaze preparatory to rolling up and exposing the whites. He will not fall, since the strike was not one of power, though his knees may buckle slightly.

If his eyes do roll-up and he collapses forward in the first ten seconds, his heart has skipped and failed to restart on the next beat impulse. Lay the subject on his back and resuscitate using the precordial thump technique of cardio-pulmonary resuscitation.

If he coughs within thirty seconds, his heart has

Figure 41

skipped and restarted as intended (figure forty-one). The reaction will be as above with these exceptions: the eyes will water, and the face will become flushed after the previous ashen color.

Be careful in selecting subjects for this experiment, since a loyal student will often try to show his prowess by not coughing. Also, those with high blood pressure are more vulnerable.

The beauty of this technique is that no bruising or trauma will develop at the point of impact, though the subject's shoulder may be a bit sore for a few days. This lack of trauma is also seen in the killing application. The strike is so slight compared to the damage inflicted that few, if any, blood vessels are ruptured; and since the heart stops immediately, no blood seeps into the muscle tissue to cause discoloration.

 # POSTSCRIPT

"Under Heaven, all can know good as good, only because there is Evil. And all can know beauty as beauty, only because there is ugliness . . . ."

So it is with the Ninja Death Touch. Man is a violent animal; so violent that when no outside threat exists to his survival, he will wage war on his neighbor for the sake of conquest. Since those of us who prize peace and harmony above all else believe that the taking of a life does no one honor, we have evolved a simple method for handling such confrontations: *leave the area.*

There are, however, those occasions when the enemy pursues or otherwise forces his own violence upon us. At these times it is taught that we should check rather than injure, injure rather than cripple, cripple rather than maim, maim rather than kill, and kill only to survive.

Yet should the need arise, and you are forced to defend yourself to the point of killing, then act with ruthless efficiency. The necessary methods are explained in this work. Ask no quarter and give none.

This is the Way of the Ninja Death Touch.